# Who Was
# Elvis Presley?

# Who Was Elvis Presley?

by Geoff Edgers

illustrated by John O'Brien

Penguin Workshop

To L + C . . . TCB—GE
For Linda—JOB

PENGUIN WORKSHOP
An Imprint of Penguin Random House LLC, New York


Published by Penguin Workshop, an imprint of Penguin Random House LLC, New York.
PENGUIN and PENGUIN WORKSHOP are trademarks of Penguin Books Ltd.
WHO HQ & Design is a registered trademark of Penguin Random House LLC.
Printed in the USA.

Visit us online at www.penguinrandomhouse.com.

Library of Congress Control Number: 2007006990

ISBN 9780448446424 40 39 38 37 36 35 34

# Contents

# Who Was Elvis Presley?

He was called "The King." That's because Elvis Presley ruled rock and roll. There were other singers in the 1950s. But nobody like Elvis. He looked different. He greased up his black hair and grew long sideburns. He wore whatever he wanted. Even pink pants with black stripes looked cool on Elvis. And, boy, could he dance.

Then there was the music. In the fifties, before Elvis, there was no rock and roll. There were two kinds of popular music. On the radio, white singers sang romantic songs or cute songs. A big hit in 1953 was "(How Much Is) That Doggie in the Window?" In small clubs, black singers were performing rhythm and blues, or R & B. It was loud, with a strong beat, and was easy to dance to. Back then, R & B wasn't played very much on radio stations—just because it was black music.

But Elvis listened to those black singers, mainly from records other kids had. And he loved that music.

Rhythm and blues music helped make Elvis a big star. He sang R & B in his own special way. Girls screamed when he stood onstage and wiggled his hips. Boys tried to look like him. Parents were upset. They didn't like this new music. They thought Elvis was too wild.

But there was no turning back. This was the start of rock and roll. And of all the rock stars to come, Elvis was always the biggest. He had one hit record after another. He sold out concerts. He became a movie star. And when he died more than thirty years ago, Elvis left behind millions of fans who still miss him. Tours of his home, Graceland, are packed.

GRACELAND

Thousands of people show up in Memphis, Tennessee, to celebrate his birthday. They are also there to cry on the anniversary of the day he died.

Elvis Presley is gone, but the King lives on.

# Chapter 1
# Tupelo

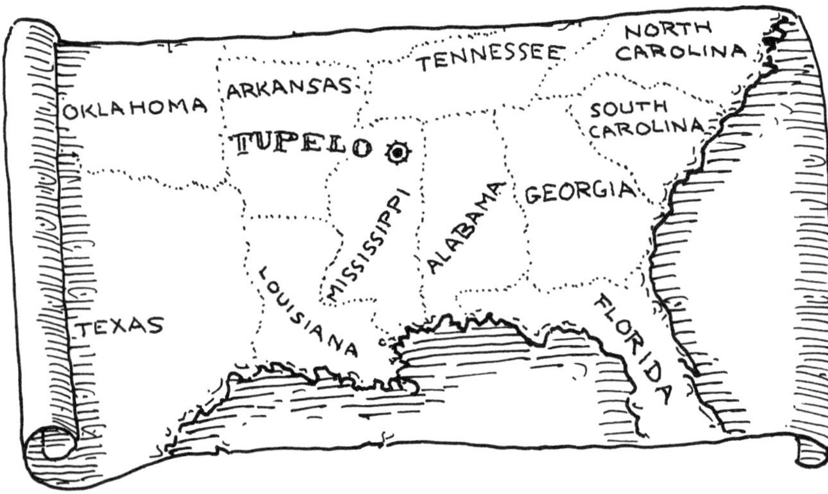


Elvis wasn't always rich. He didn't always own a mansion or a garage filled with Cadillacs. He didn't always have fancy clothes and expensive jewelry.

As a boy, Elvis was poor. Very poor.

Elvis Aron Presley was born on January 8, 1935, in Tupelo, Mississippi. His mother, Gladys, was pregnant with twins, but she didn't know it. Like a lot of poor people in the South, the Presleys didn't have the money to see doctors. So Elvis's mother gave birth at home.

The delivery was difficult. At around four in the morning, Gladys gave birth to a son, but sadly he was stillborn. Then Gladys realized there was another baby still inside her. About a half hour later, Elvis arrived. The family named the baby who died Jesse Garon. The healthy boy was named Elvis Aron. Gladys and Vernon Presley couldn't even afford a gravestone for little Jesse Garon.

Though he never met Jesse Garon, Elvis thought about his twin all the time. He wondered what life would have been like with a brother. As a boy, he would go visit Jesse's grave. As a famous rock star, Elvis still talked about the brother he never knew.

Elvis's childhood wasn't easy. His family struggled. The Presleys lived on the poor side of town. Their house had only two rooms.

Vernon hadn't finished high school. He married Gladys when he was just seventeen. Without an education, Vernon found it hard to find or keep a good job. At different times he worked on farms, painted houses, and drove trucks.

A lot of people were going through hard times, just like the Presleys. Elvis was born in the middle of the Great Depression. All across the United States, people couldn't find work. They couldn't make enough money for food and clothes. People had to beg for food, or hope for free lunch at a soup kitchen. Families moved from town to town looking for work. Some people had to live in cardboard boxes.

At least the Presleys had a home. It didn't have electricity or running water. There was no indoor bathroom. Instead, Vernon built an outhouse in the backyard. An outhouse is a small, wood hut

with no real toilet. Just a hole in the ground.

Gladys couldn't have any more babies. So she became very nervous that Elvis might get hurt.

She walked him to school every day. She gave him a whipping when he did something wrong. Elvis didn't like getting hit, but he loved his mother very much. He would hurry home after school in the afternoon to be with Mama.

The Presley family went through ups and downs. When Vernon got a good job, the family would usually buy a new house. When he lost a job, they would have to sell it and move into a smaller, rented place. One time Vernon was so desperate, he tried to cheat someone out of money. That got him in big trouble. A judge sent Vernon to jail for eight months. Gladys and Elvis were forced to move in with Vernon's family.

Most weekends, they rode a bus to see Vernon in prison. It was ten hours round-trip. Elvis, who was just three, sometimes sat on the front steps of his house, crying. He didn't think his father would ever come home.

But Vernon did return, and he found a new job. The family joined a local church. It was at church that Elvis first started singing. He was so good that he sang with the choir. Right away, people could tell that his voice was special. He even won a prize at a fair for singing. Gladys always encouraged Elvis. The family couldn't afford much. However, for Elvis's eleventh birthday, Gladys gave him his first guitar.

"It will help you with your singing," she told him. "And everyone does enjoy hearing you sing."

# GRAND OLE OPRY

BACK BEFORE IPODS OR CDS, PEOPLE LISTENED TO MUSIC AT HOME ON RECORD PLAYERS OR ON THE RADIO. RADIO SHOWS WERE POPULAR THE WAY TV SHOWS ARE NOW.

IN 1925 A NASHVILLE RADIO STATION BEGAN HOSTING CONCERTS FEATURING THE BIGGEST COUNTRY MUSIC STARS. THE SHOW WAS FIRST NAMED THE *WSM BARN DANCE.* TWO YEARS LATER, IT BECAME KNOWN AS THE *GRAND OLE OPRY.* EVERY WEEK, CROWDS FILLED THE HALLWAYS OF THE STATION TO HEAR HANK WILLIAMS, MINNIE PEARL, AND OTHERS. THE SHOW WAS SO POPULAR, IT MOVED INTO AN AUDITORIUM, AND THEN INTO AN EVEN BIGGER ONE.

TODAY, COUNTRY MUSIC FANS CAN HEAR THE SHOWS ON THE RADIO OR WATCH THEM ON TELEVISION. ELVIS LOVED LISTENING TO THE *OPRY* AS A KID. HE PERFORMED ON THE SHOW ONLY ONCE, ON OCTOBER 2, 1954.

## Chapter 2
## Memphis

Now that Elvis had a guitar, he wanted to play it. Gladys asked a local pastor named Frank Smith to help teach her son the guitar. Elvis was his own teacher, too. By reading a book, he figured

out where to put his fingers. Elvis began hanging out at WELO, the local radio station. There, he heard older and better guitar players. He listened carefully to how they played. And every Saturday night, Elvis, Gladys, and Vernon would gather around their radio. They listened to the songs of country music stars from the *Grand Ole Opry*.

"I took the guitar and I watched people, and I learned to play a little bit," Elvis said later. "But I would never sing in public. I was very shy about it, you know."

In seventh grade, Elvis started to bring his guitar to school every day—except when it was raining. Some kids made fun of him. They called his songs "hillbilly music." "Hillbilly" was a nasty name for someone who lived in the backwoods. Some kids were even meaner. One cut the strings off Elvis's guitar when he wasn't looking.

In November of 1948, when Elvis was in the middle of eighth grade, Vernon and Gladys decided to move again. But this time, they weren't heading to another shack in Tupelo. No, the

Presleys were headed to the big city: Memphis, Tennessee. It was a little more than one hundred miles away. They packed the family car, a 1939 Plymouth, and left. They were looking for a fresh start. And they got it. Before long, Vernon had a job loading and unloading heavy cases of paint. Gladys worked in a factory that made curtains.

Elvis needed a new guitar teacher. He found one in Jesse Lee, the eighteen-year-old son of the local preacher. Every Saturday and Sunday, Jesse Lee came over to the Presley home. He and Elvis practiced downstairs in the laundry room.

In Memphis, Elvis began to grow up. The shy kid made friends: Buzzy, Farley, and Paul. The four boys rode bikes together, went to the movies, and played football. They made money mowing lawns.

By his junior year in high school, Elvis looked different. He grew sideburns, which made him look older. He also started meeting girls. They

liked the fact that he was still a little shy. Elvis took a girl named Regis to the school prom.

Then there was music. Memphis was so much bigger than Tupelo. Elvis went to Charlie's, a store where kids were allowed to hang out and listen to records. In those days there were no iPods or CDs. Elvis and his buddies put on 78s, records made of thick shellac. Only one song fit on each side. Elvis visited the local radio station, WMPS, which would host concerts. He also went to Ellis Auditorium. Once a month, people gathered there to sing gospel songs, the music Elvis knew from church. Sometimes, they sang all through the night.

At parties, the once bashful Elvis started to loosen up. But he was still shy. His Aunt Lillian described how her nephew once sang at

a birthday party. "I moved everything out of the living room, and Elvis [came] in and brought his guitar," remembered Lillian. "But we had to put the lights out before he'd sing."

Shy or not, singing was Elvis's great love. And he was living in Memphis at just the right time. Memphis was home to Sun Studios, a company started by a man named Sam Phillips.

Mr. Phillips, as Elvis called him, wanted to record a new kind of music. It didn't have a name. It used the electric guitar, and the singing—or vocals—was loud. The music was faster than what was played on the radio, and more fun to dance to. Nobody knew what to call it, but years later it became known as "rock and roll." At first, many of the musicians recording for Mr. Phillips were black: singers named Howlin' Wolf and Rufus Thomas.

Then, in August of 1953, eighteen-year-old Elvis walked into Sun Studios. Shyly, he put

$3.98 on the table. He wanted to record a song for his mother. And so Elvis Presley stepped into the recording studio for the first time.

# GOSPEL MUSIC

IF YOU DIDN'T LISTEN TO THE WORDS, YOU MIGHT NOT REALIZE THE DIFFERENCE BETWEEN EARLY ROCK AND ROLL AND GOSPEL. SINGERS SANG LOUDLY AND WITH LOTS OF FEELING. THEY MIGHT GET SO SWEPT UP IN THE MOMENT, THEY WOULD SCREAM. BUT GOSPEL IS SPECIAL RELIGIOUS MUSIC. IT GREW OUT OF BLACK CHURCH CHOIRS IN THE EARLY 1900S.

AS A BOY, ELVIS GREW TO LOVE GOSPEL MUSIC FROM HIS SUNDAY CHURCH VISITS. HE HEARD FAMOUS GOSPEL SINGERS SUCH AS SISTER ROSETTA THARPE WHEN HE WAS GROWING UP. EVEN AFTER ELVIS BECAME A ROCK STAR, HE SOMETIMES RECORDED GOSPEL SONGS. HE WON A GRAMMY AWARD FOR HIS 1967 RECORD *HOW GREAT THOU ART.*

## Chapter 3
## Sun Studios

Elvis went to Sun Studios with his beat-up guitar. The song he chose to sing, "My Happiness," had been popular a few years earlier. It was a soft ballad that his mother loved.

A nice woman named Marion Keisker ran Sun Records with Mr. Phillips. From behind her desk, she asked Elvis what kind of music he sang.

"I sing all kinds," he told her.

"Who do you sound like?" she asked.

"I don't sound like nobody," Elvis told her.

Elvis recorded "My Happiness." Mrs. Keisker printed his name out and pasted it onto the record. Elvis left.

But he came back.

In fact, Elvis kept on visiting Sun. Mr. Phillips was always too busy to talk with him. Mrs. Keisker, though, loved to chat with the handsome boy who had the voice of an angel.

Elvis had graduated high school by this time. Like a lot of people he knew, he didn't plan on going to college. Instead, he got a job at a machine shop. And he sang.

Elvis kept going to all-night gospel sing-alongs. He listened to the radio so he could learn how to play more songs. One night, Elvis heard about a band looking for a singer. This could be his big break! He got a special haircut and wore a pink shirt for the tryout. Elvis sang only two songs. A friend of his watched. Afterward, he told Elvis, "You're never going to make it as a singer."

If only he knew.

One day in the summer of 1954, Mrs. Keisker called Elvis. Mr. Phillips had a song that might be right for Elvis. Could Elvis get down to the studio that afternoon?

Of course he could! But it turned out that Mr. Phillips didn't like how Elvis sang the song. He asked Elvis if he knew any others. Sure, he did. Elvis sang every song he knew. Then he sang parts of songs he knew. Mr. Phillips stopped recording and just sat in the recording booth, listening. He knew this kid didn't have experience. He knew Elvis needed training. But Mr. Phillips also knew that Elvis had something very special.

Mr. Phillips told a local guitar player about Elvis. His name was Scotty Moore, and he wanted to hear Elvis. But when he called, Elvis wasn't home. That didn't stop Gladys. She rushed to the movie theater where Elvis was, to tell him the news.

A few days later, Elvis went over to Scotty's house. Scotty thought the boy looked a little crazy. Elvis was wearing pink pants, white shoes, and a black shirt. And his hair was greased up in a style called a "ducktail." Scotty introduced Elvis to his friend Bill, who played bass guitar. A regular guitar has six strings. A bass has only four and makes a deeper sound.

Again, Elvis played every song he knew. Most of the songs were slow ballads. Neither Scotty nor Bill was impressed. But they agreed to go into the studio with Elvis the next night.

At Sun Studios, with the other two musicians, Elvis sang "I Love You Because" every which way. Sometimes he let his voice go high, sometimes low. Sometimes he whistled during it, sometimes he didn't. Unfortunately, Mr. Phillips wasn't happy with any of these recordings. He told everybody to take a break.

The two guitar players got sodas. But Elvis kept fiddling with his guitar. All of a sudden, he started playing an old blues song. It was called "That's All Right [Mama]." As he sang, Elvis started dancing and jumping around the room. The guitarists heard Elvis and liked what he was doing. They put down their sodas and started to play along.

At last, Mr. Phillips was hearing something he liked.

When everybody in the studio listened to the recording, they were amazed. It was loud and electric and different. Mr. Phillips called the local radio station and asked the disc jockey to put on

the record. When "That's All Right [Mama]" played the next night, Gladys and Vernon were standing close to the radio so they could really listen to their son. Others must have really listened, too, because more than one hundred people called the radio station to play that song again.

It wasn't long before Elvis, Scotty, and the bass player began appearing at local concerts. People loved to hear Elvis sing, but they loved to watch him, too. He was so handsome, and when he shook his hips, girls went wild.

At the end of one show, Elvis joked with his fans, saying, "Girls, I'll see you backstage."

That was all they needed to hear.

Screaming girls pushed through an open window into his dressing room. They tore off his shirt and boots and tried to yank off his pants. Elvis held on tight. Only a few months before, Elvis was driving a truck to make money. That night, he started to feel like a star.

# ACOUSTIC AND ELECTRIC GUITARS

THEY EACH HAVE SIX STRINGS. BUT THERE'S A BIG DIFFERENCE BETWEEN ACOUSTIC AND ELECTRIC GUITARS.

AN ACOUSTIC GUITAR HAS A HOLLOW BODY AND A SOUND HOLE. THAT'S THE CIRCLE UNDER THE PART YOU STRUM. WHEN YOU PLUCK THE STRINGS, THE SOUND VIBRATES OFF THEM AND INTO THE HOLLOW BODY THROUGH THAT HOLE. ELECTRIC GUITARS WORK DIFFERENTLY. INSTEAD OF A HOLLOW BODY, MOST ELECTRIC GUITARS ARE FULL OF WIRES TO TRANSMIT SOUNDS. A PLUCK OF THE STRINGS GOES THROUGH A CORD INTO A SPEAKER. THIS MAKES THE GUITAR LOUD ENOUGH TO BE HEARD BY SOMEBODY STANDING IN THE BACK ROW OF A GIANT STADIUM.

ELVIS USUALLY PLAYED AN ACOUSTIC GUITAR. YOU CAN HEAR HIM STRUM ON "BLUE MOON OF KENTUCKY." SCOTTY MOORE, HIS GUITARIST IN THE SUN STUDIOS YEARS, PLAYED ELECTRIC GUITAR. USING AN AMPLIFIER, MOORE OFTEN ADDED AN ECHO EFFECT TO HIS GUITAR. MOORE BECAME FAMOUS FOR THAT "REVERB" SOUND.

## Chapter 4
## Colonel Tom Parker

Girls weren't the only ones interested in watching Elvis. A man named Colonel Tom Parker also took note. Colonel Parker wasn't actually a colonel. He had once been in the army, but he was not an

COLONEL TOM PARKER

officer. And he dropped out to join the circus. Parker thought "colonel" made him sound important. Parker couldn't sing or play an instrument. He was a businessman who managed country singer Hank Snow.

Colonel Parker had big plans for Elvis. When they met, he told the young singer that playing small concerts near his home wasn't good enough. He should be touring the country. Elvis should appear on television shows, and star in movies. With his looks and style, Elvis could be bigger than anyone before him.

There was one problem. Elvis already had a manager. His name was Bob Neal. Bob was friendly and hard-working. He got Elvis a regular spot on the *Louisiana Hayride*, a popular concert series on the radio. He also helped Elvis make business deals with Mr. Phillips at Sun Studios.

But that didn't stop Parker. He was pushy. Parker knew Elvis needed him. Sun was too small.

Bob Neal was too small, and Elvis was going to be big. Famous record companies should be recording his music. That was the way to get big hits heard all across the country.

Mr. Phillips knew all of this, too. But he didn't like Parker, and he didn't want to let Elvis go.

Vernon wanted Elvis to sign with Parker. The talk of movies and big record deals impressed Elvis's father. But Gladys had her doubts. She hardly knew this Colonel Parker. And he wasn't easy to like. Parker smoked big cigars that stank up their home. He was older than Vernon. He was blunt, saying whatever he wanted, even if it made people feel bad. He only seemed to care about money.

Gladys worried about girls running after her son, tearing at his clothes. Would he be happy spending most nights on a bus, traveling from concert to concert? Gladys wanted him to settle down and start a family.

Elvis adored his mama. Still, he ended up doing what his father wanted. In August of 1955, Colonel Parker became "special adviser" to Elvis. And, sure enough, a few months later, Parker got RCA Records to buy Elvis's contract with Sun. RCA paid thirty-five thousand dollars. That was more money than any other record company had ever paid for a singer. Some people at RCA worried that Elvis would be a flop. Maybe they had made a big mistake.

They had nothing to worry about.

# Chapter 5
# "Hound Dog"

Elvis's first song for RCA was about a man whose girlfriend had broken up with him. The song was slow and depressing. But Elvis sang it his way. His voice was low and quiet in parts. At other times, he shouted. The sound was raw and full of feeling. Unlike other rock songs, it wasn't fast or easy to dance to. People liked it anyway. "Heartbreak Hotel" soon came to be the most popular song in the country.

That's how 1956 started for Elvis. He was just twenty-one, but he was about to change music forever. Fame was going to change his life, too. After "Heartbreak Hotel," Elvis had money—lots of money. He bought Gladys a

pink Cadillac and a new house for the Presleys with a swimming pool.

Why did Elvis get so popular so fast?

Television helped. Back in those days, there were only a few channels and a few popular shows. When Elvis appeared on TV, people couldn't believe what they were seeing. Popular singers didn't wear tight jeans and tight shirts! Nobody else had a greasy ducktail.

Elvis got swept up in the music as he sang. His knees would shake; he'd curl his lip in a sneer. Then he'd smile a little and shut his eyes. He'd also move his hips back and forth. Grown-ups thought this was dirty dancing. People started to call him "Elvis the Pelvis." They didn't want their kids to watch Elvis or to dress like him.

"Mr. Presley has no discernible singing ability," *The New York Times* wrote.

Another newspaper had a headline that read: "Beware Elvis Presley." What people said hurt Elvis. He wasn't wild. He still lived with his mom and dad. He just wanted to sing and make people

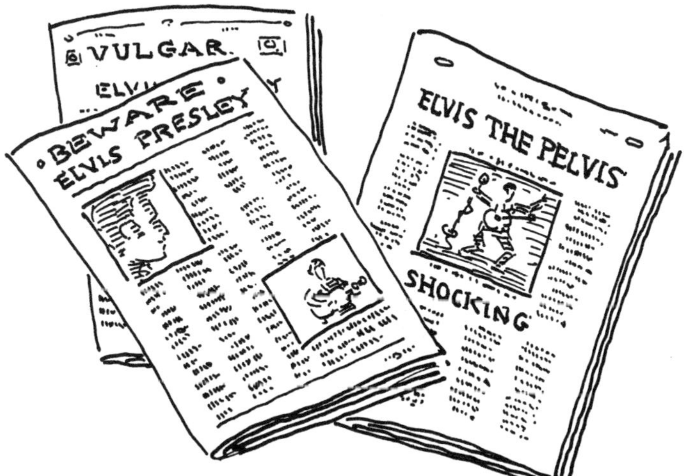

happy. "I don't do any vulgar movements," Elvis said to reporters. "It's just my way of expressing how I feel."

Steve Allen, a famous TV host, had Elvis wear a tuxedo on his show. He told Elvis not to shake his hips. Instead, Allen had Elvis sing his song "Hound Dog" to a basset hound also wearing a tuxedo. *The Ed Sullivan Show* was a popular

Sunday night show. When Elvis came on, the cameras showed him only from the waist up. If he wiggled his hips or shook his legs, the viewers wouldn't see it.

In the end, it didn't matter what grown-ups thought of Elvis. The time was ripe for Elvis

Presley. This was the late 1950s. Some young people were starting to rebel against their parents. Rock and roll was their music. Frank Sinatra was their parents' singer. Elvis was theirs. After "Heartbreak Hotel," the hits kept coming. "Hound Dog" and "Don't Be Cruel" went straight to number one.

Elvis Presley didn't create rock and roll. Bill Haley had a big hit with "Rock Around the Clock." Chuck Berry, famous for his "duck walk" across the stage, sang "Johnny B. Goode." And

CHUCK BERRY

JERRY LEE LEWIS

Jerry Lee Lewis, who sometimes kicked away his piano bench when he played, was another rock-and-roll star. But Elvis, with his looks and voice, was much bigger than anybody else.

For Colonel Parker, Elvis still wasn't big enough. He wanted Elvis to be King. And to do that, Elvis needed to be in movies.

## Chapter 6
## Movie Star

Once again, Elvis's timing was right. The young actor James Dean had died in a car accident in 1955. Elvis was a great fan of

Dean's. He had seen *Rebel Without a Cause* more than forty times. James Dean and Elvis Presley were both young, handsome, and sexy.

Movie producers were desperate to find the next James Dean. They thought Elvis might do the trick. Elvis signed a deal with a big Hollywood movie studio. In 1956, he arrived on the set of *Love Me Tender*. It took place during the Civil War. Elvis played a singing farmboy.

Movie critics didn't like *Love Me Tender*. Elvis didn't know the first thing about acting. How could he? He'd never done it before. They also thought it was silly for his character to sing in the middle of scenes. Colonel Parker didn't care about the critics—neither did fans. *Love Me Tender* was a big hit. Elvis's fans filled up theaters, many fans seeing the movie again and again.

The movie people were excited. Here was their new James Dean. They were willing to pay a lot of

money to keep Elvis Presley. Before long, Elvis was making one movie after another. He made thirty-one between 1956 and 1969.

Making movies kept Elvis so busy, he barely had time to record music. He certainly didn't have time for concerts. Colonel Parker didn't mind. Why did Elvis need to tour? His records sold even if he didn't appear before an audience.

In 1957 Elvis bought a mansion in Memphis. He called it Graceland. He planned for the whole family to live there. But in less than a year, something happened.

Elvis was drafted. Today, people decide whether to join the armed forces. But before 1973, men had no choice. They had to serve. (Women were not drafted.) Not even Elvis Presley could avoid the draft. And even Elvis had to get an army crew cut. "Before" and "after" photos of Elvis made newspaper headlines all over the country.

Elvis was no longer a rock star. He was Private Elvis Presley.

Then something terrible happened.

Gladys became very sick. She couldn't eat anything and had to go into the hospital. Elvis kept her pink Cadillac parked right outside her window so she could see it from bed. Elvis was allowed to come home to visit her. For a while, Gladys seemed better. Then, in the middle of the night, the doctors called Elvis. He rushed off to the hospital. But his mother had died before he got there.

It was the biggest loss of his life. Gladys hadn't just been his mother. She was his best friend, the person closest to him in the whole world.

TV

The next morning, Elvis sat on the front step of his beautiful new house and cried. But because he was Elvis, there was no privacy. Photographers snapped pictures of him weeping into his hands.

# GRACELAND

EVEN THOUGH HIS MOTHER HAD DIED, ELVIS KEPT THE HOUSE, WHICH SAT ON FOURTEEN ACRES OF LAND IN MEMPHIS. THERE WERE WHITE COLUMNS OUTSIDE, A MARBLE FIREPLACE IN THE FRONT HALL, AND EIGHT BATHROOMS. THE HOUSE LOOKED JUST THE WAY ELVIS WANTED. "THE JUNGLE ROOM" HAD JUNGLE FLOWERS AND PLANTS, BAMBOO WALLS, AND WILD-ANIMAL PRINTS ON THE FURNITURE. GRACELAND ALSO HAD A RACQUETBALL COURT, A ROOM FOR ELVIS'S GOLD RECORDS

AND AWARDS, AND A GARAGE FULL OF ANTIQUE CARS. HE EVEN KEPT TWO PLANES ON THE PROPERTY, ONE OF THEM NAMED AFTER HIS DAUGHTER, LISA MARIE.

IN 1976 BRUCE SPRINGSTEEN WANTED TO MEET ELVIS SO MUCH, HE CLIMBED THE WALLS AT GRACELAND. GUARDS CAUGHT HIM AND SENT HIM AWAY. ELVIS WASN'T HOME!

TODAY, NOBODY IN THE PRESLEY FAMILY LIVES THERE. BUT THE HOUSE IS OPEN FOR TOURS.

# Chapter 7
# Priscilla

Private Presley was sent to an army base in Friedberg, Germany, on October 1, 1958. Elvis thought he would never be happy again. His mother was gone. And he was thousands of miles from home.

Meanwhile, Colonel Parker had other worries. What would being in the army do to Elvis Presley's career?

The United States was not at war, so Elvis never fought in any battles. Army bases near enemy countries, such as the USSR, were there in case of war. In Germany, Elvis drove a Jeep for a sergeant. He and a friend were also in charge of a talent show. Elvis played piano. Still, Elvis wasn't treated

NORTH SEA
DENMARK
SWEDEN
GREAT BRITAIN
NETHERLANDS
GERMANY
POLAND
BELGIUM
FRIEDBERG
LUX.
CZECH REPUBLIC
FRANCE
SWITZERLAND
AUSTRIA
HUNGARY
SLOVENIA
ITALY
CROATIA
BOSNIA HERZEGOVINA
MEDITERRANEAN SEA

like just any soldier who had to sleep on a bunk bed in the barracks.

Elvis rented rooms at a local hotel. His grandma and father flew over for a visit. Elvis invited two friends from Memphis, too.

During the day, Elvis had to work. But at night, he and his two buddies loved to goof around. They ran through the hotel shooting squirt guns. One time a prank went too far: They set a small fire by mistake, and the hotel manager kicked them out. After that, Elvis rented a house.

Elvis started to get by on less and less sleep. The only time for fun was at night. But he needed to be awake during the day. Another soldier gave Elvis pills to help him stay awake. The pills worked. So he began to take more. In those days, nobody really understood the danger of such pills. Once people started taking them, they couldn't stop.

After his father and friends returned to Memphis, Elvis was lonelier than ever. But then Elvis met Priscilla Beaulieu. She was an American girl who was fourteen-and-a-half years old. Elvis was twenty-four. Priscilla's stepfather was a captain in the air force. He said

PRISCILLA BEAULIEU

she was too young to go on a date. But Elvis went to visit Priscilla's stepfather. He promised to remain

just friends with Priscilla. He would wait until she was older before starting a romance. For the first time, he thought he was in love.

In March of 1960, the army sent Elvis home. He had served for more than a year. At the airport, Priscilla said goodbye for now. She worried that they'd never see each other again. But Elvis loved her. He told her so in all his letters to her.

Now that Elvis was back in the United States, Colonel Parker focused on his career again. Elvis was going to be bigger than ever. The famous singer Frank Sinatra hosted a television program

to welcome Elvis home. That was on March 26, 1960. Elvis sang two songs. Girls in the audience screamed throughout his performance.

The King was back.

## Chapter 8
## Elvis Flops

Elvis started making the same silly movies again, starting with *G.I. Blues.* Though he longed to make a great film, he played a singing lifeguard in *Fun in Acapulco*, a singing race-car driver in *Spinout*, and a singing doctor who falls in love with a nun in

*Change of Habit*. Still, people kept buying tickets for Elvis Presley movies. The songs in the movies were good. There was "Can't Help Falling in Love" in a 1961 movie called *Blue Hawaii*. It remains a classic love ballad. The next year, he had another hit with "Return to Sender" from the movie *Girls! Girls! Girls!*

In real life, the only girl in his life was Priscilla. She and Elvis were reunited when she left Germany and came back to the United States.

The couple was married on May 1, 1967, at the Aladdin Hotel, in Las Vegas. Less than a year later, on February 1, 1968, their daughter Lisa Marie was born.

But the happy times didn't last. Colonel Parker was working Elvis too hard. With an overloaded schedule, Elvis never had time for acting lessons. Sometimes he didn't start learning his lines until he was in the car driving to the movie set.

His movie schedule also prevented him from recording new music. There wasn't time to spend recording in a studio. And young people's tastes were changing. It was the 1960s. People were listening to Bob Dylan, the Beatles, the Rolling Stones. Folk singers were protesting the Vietnam War and racism. Then there was Elvis. He sang "Old MacDonald (Had a Farm)" in a terrible movie called *Double Trouble*. He seemed to belong to the past.

BOB DYLAN

Elvis's biggest fear was coming true. He was only thirty-two and no longer popular—not the way he had been before. People didn't take him seriously. Elvis felt trapped and jealous. When the Beatles came to his house to meet him, at first Elvis barely looked up at the younger musicians. He pretended to keep watching TV. In the end, they did "jam" together on a couple of songs.

Elvis grew more and more depressed. All the work made it hard for him to get much rest. Once again, Elvis got in the habit of taking pills to stay awake. Then, when he needed rest, he took other pills to go to sleep. Elvis started staying up all night and then sleeping through the days. All the drugs made him puffy, and he started to gain weight. Worst of all, he and Priscilla, the wife he loved so much, started to argue a lot.

He needed something to inspire him. He needed a goal. He needed to make a comeback.

## Chapter 9
## The Comeback

It was 1968. Elvis knew his career needed changes. He had to break away from Colonel Parker. That wouldn't be easy. His father still believed in Parker. Vernon wondered why Elvis was so upset. Elvis had it all: a mansion, private planes, a beautiful wife, and a baby girl.

But Elvis was unhappy. He wanted to play concerts again. He wanted to hear screaming fans. He missed making good music. Forget the Beatles and the Rolling Stones. He was the King. It was time to remind everyone of that.

The big comeback began on television. In 1968, NBC signed up Elvis to do a TV special. NBC hired a good director and writers to put together the program. Colonel Parker was barely involved.

The show was going to remind everybody why they loved Elvis. He was going to be up onstage again, flashing that famous smile. He was going to sing with the same boldness as in his early days on TV. It would be classic Elvis. No songs like "Old MacDonald."

Elvis was ready. He exercised to get in shape. He grew long sideburns again. He had a tight, black leather suit made for the show. And his old friend Scotty Moore, from the Sun recording days, was going to play with him. There was a studio audience, so it would feel like a real concert.

Then, right before the start of the show, Elvis got nervous. Really nervous. It had been so long since he had performed in front of anybody.

Still, Elvis took the stage. He sang new songs and old songs. He played "Hound Dog" and "That's All Right [Mama]." He was happy and handsome and smooth and electric. He was great that night. The Elvis special was the most popular show of the season.

# THE ELVIS JUMPSUITS

MAYBE IT WAS BECAUSE, AS A BOY, HE COULD BARELY AFFORD SHOES, BUT ELVIS, THE ROCK STAR, LOVED FANCY CLOTHES. BEGINNING IN 1957, A HOLLYWOOD DESIGNER NAMED NUDIE COHEN MADE MANY WILD OUTFITS FOR ELVIS. THE MOST FAMOUS WAS A GOLD LAMÉ JUMPSUIT. IT COST TEN THOUSAND DOLLARS—MORE EXPENSIVE THAN A CAR AT THE TIME.

FOR ELVIS'S TV COMEBACK IN 1968, A DESIGNER NAMED BILL BELEW MADE A BLACK LEATHER SUIT FOR THE KING. IN THE 1970S, BELEW DESIGNED JUMPSUITS FOR ELVIS.

THEY HAD THICK BELTS AND PANTS THAT FLARED WAY OUT AT THE BOTTOM. MANY WERE STUDDED WITH JEWELS. BELEW GAVE THE SUITS NAMES. "BURNING FLAME OF LOVE" WAS FIRE RED. "ALOHA" HAD A GIANT EAGLE ON THE BACK, AND A CAPE.

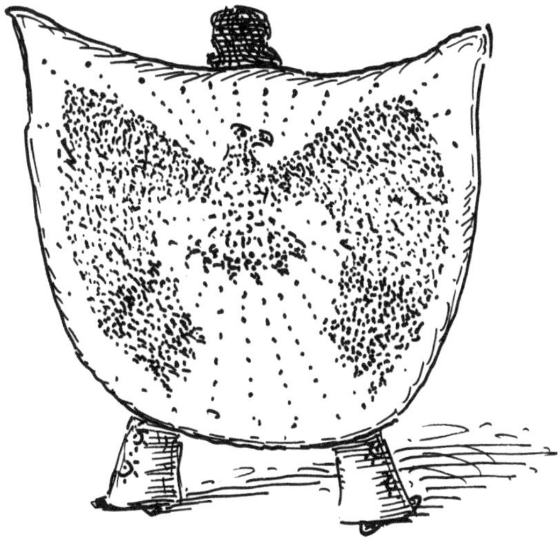

BELEW STILL MAKES JUMPSUITS THAT SELL FOR AS MUCH AS FIVE THOUSAND DOLLARS. BELEW'S COMPANY ALSO MAKES SHINY, SILVER-AND-DIAMOND RINGS DECORATED WITH THE LETTERS *TCB*. THAT STANDS FOR "TAKIN' CARE OF BUSINESS." IT WAS ELVIS'S SLOGAN.

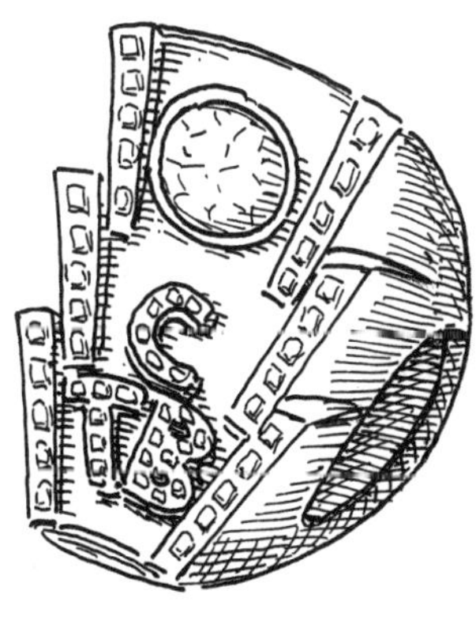

But the comeback wasn't complete.

Elvis needed to make new music. He wanted to compete with the Beatles. In January of 1969, Elvis went to a new producer. His name was Chips Moman. Chips wasn't like other people around Elvis. Chips didn't worry about upsetting the King. He said what he felt.

CHIPS MOMAN

When a recording wasn't good enough, he had a simple way of dealing with it. Chips would say, "Try it again, Elvis."

And Elvis never argued. He wanted to make great music.

Elvis never wrote his own songs; he had to choose what to sing. With Chips, he stayed away from light songs like the ones in his movies. Chips suggested a song called “In the Ghetto.” It was about African-American children living in poor neighborhoods.

Many of Elvis's friends told him not to make message songs. That wasn't Elvis's image. But Elvis trusted Chips. And "In the Ghetto" became a big hit.

Another song was about a man and a woman breaking up. In "Suspicious Minds" there were horns and women singing backup and a groovy electric-guitar part. The song had slow parts and fast parts. Elvis floated through all of them. When "Suspicious Minds" came out in August 1969, it went straight up the charts. Elvis had

his first number one hit in seven years.

But the comeback still wasn't complete.

Elvis wanted to play concerts again. For this, he needed Colonel Parker's help. Parker made a deal for Elvis to appear for several weeks at a giant hotel in Las Vegas. Now Elvis could sing in front of fans, but he wouldn't have to travel all over the country to perform.

Once again, right before his first show, Elvis

got nervous. He paced around backstage. He worried that people would be disappointed.

Boy, was he wrong. In just a few weeks, Elvis sold more than one hundred thousand tickets. In one year Elvis had made a dramatic comeback. He was a star on television, radio, and stage again.

# LAS VEGAS

IT IS A STRANGE PLACE FOR A CITY: THE CENTER OF THE MOJAVE DESERT. THE CITY ONLY EXISTS BECAUSE OF WATER FROM THE HOOVER DAM. AND GAMBLING THERE IS LEGAL. IN MOST OTHER CITIES, IT IS AGAINST THE LAW. GAMBLING LED TO THE BUILDING OF GIANT CASINOS AND HOTELS. THESE DAYS, LAS VEGAS ATTRACTS ALMOST FORTY MILLION VISITORS EACH YEAR.

THE BIGGEST HOTELS AND CASINOS IN LAS VEGAS ARE ON "THE STRIP," WITH ITS FLASHING NEON SIGNS. THE DESERT HEAT KEEPS PEOPLE INDOORS, WHERE THEY CAN GAMBLE, SHOP, EAT, AND SEE BIG SHOWS.

IN THE 1970S, THE BIGGEST SHOW OF ALL WAS ELVIS'S. HE STARTED HIS CONCERT COMEBACK THERE IN 1969. OVER THE YEARS, ELVIS KEPT GOING BACK TO LAS VEGAS. SOME OF HIS CONCERTS WERE BROADCAST ON TV. EVEN NOW, THEY ARE SOMETIMES RERUN.

## Chapter 10
## Downhill

It was a great comeback. The string of sold-out concerts and hit records jump-started Elvis Presley's career. He was incredibly popular again. In 1973, another Elvis TV special made history. *Aloha from Hawaii* was shown in forty countries to more than one billion people.

But his personal problems didn't go away.

For a little while, Elvis had done things his way. He had fought hard to make the 1968 comeback special and to sing songs that Colonel Parker didn't think were right for him.

Now Elvis was working harder than ever. He began to wear out. And when he got more tired, he found it harder to resist Colonel Parker. Deep down, he also believed they were a team. Elvis never forgot how Colonel Parker had kept his career alive while he was in Germany. Colonel Parker took control again.

Elvis performed more than 1,100 concerts from 1969 to 1977. Elvis's marriage had been strained for many years. Now it fell apart. In 1973, Elvis and Priscilla got divorced.

More and more, Elvis depended on the members of "the Memphis Mafia." This was the nickname for guys Elvis called friends.

The members of the Memphis Mafia spent all their time at Graceland. Why not? Elvis had so much money that he would buy them cars or motorcycles. In return, they kept Elvis company.

The plain truth is, Elvis was a drug addict. His body needed the pills to get through each day. Elvis should have gotten help for himself. Instead, he got angry whenever anyone suggested he had a problem. His friends also didn't push hard enough. They were scared of saying something he didn't want to hear. Elvis had a bad temper. The guys also liked the way things were. They didn't want the fun to end.

Elvis started acting strange. One time, in December 1970, he decided he had to see President Richard Nixon. So Elvis hopped on a plane and headed straight for Washington, D.C. At the White House, he demanded a meeting. Sure enough, he got one. President Nixon met with Elvis that very night.

As the 1970s wore on, Elvis grew sicker. He had never taken care of himself. He ate too much junk food. He loved milk shakes and fried peanut-butter-and-banana sandwiches. He rarely exercised. All his bad

habits started catching up with him.

Again, he gained a lot of weight. His face got puffy, and he couldn't fit into clothes. This embarrassed Elvis. He began to struggle onstage. Sometimes, he forgot the words to his most famous songs. Other times, Elvis had to miss a concert. One time he stomped off the stage in the middle of a show. In 1973 Elvis collapsed and had to go to the hospital.

Life went on like this for a few years. No one stepped in to stop it. The Elvis everybody knew was gone. What fans saw now was a broken man. Overweight, lonely, unable to remember words to his own songs.

Elvis's nights were like other people's days. One night, Elvis returned to Graceland after a 10:30 P.M. visit to the dentist. Elvis called some friends to come over.

Around four in the morning, Elvis and a friend tried playing racquetball. But the game didn't last long. Elvis was too out of shape. It was almost morning. When Elvis couldn't fall asleep, someone gave him some sleeping pills. They didn't work. So he took more.

He was found dead in his bathroom the next day. The date was August 16, 1977.

"What am I going to do?" cried Vernon, learning his son was dead. "Everything is gone."

It was such a sad, terrible end to Elvis Presley's

life. Lisa Marie was just nine. She would grow up without her father.

And then there were the fans. Elvis left behind millions of them. And year after year, there were new fans. Many were born after he died. They only know the King from records and TV reruns. As recently as 2002, a new release of Elvis's hits sold more than any other collection in the country. By some counts, Elvis has sold close to one billion albums.

Elvis is buried on the grounds of Graceland. The graves of his parents lie nearby his. So does

MINNIE MAE PRESLEY
ELVIS PRESLEY
VERNON ELVIS PRESLEY
GLADYS LOVE PRESLEY

the grave of little Jesse Garon, the twin he never knew.

Every year, on the anniversary of his death, fans crowd into Memphis to remember their idol. In 2006 the Japanese prime minister was visiting the United States. He had one request. He

asked President George W. Bush if he could visit Graceland. Lisa Marie and Priscilla Presley gave a private tour. Being there was like a dream, the Japanese prime minister said. Then he began to sing one of Elvis's songs.

# ELVIS SIGHTINGS

DID ELVIS REALLY DIE? YES. BUT SOME PEOPLE REFUSE TO BELIEVE IT. THAT'S WHY THERE ARE ELVIS "SIGHTINGS." PEOPLE ARE SURE THEY'VE SEEN THE KING. HE'S BEEN SPOTTED IN A GAS STATION IN KANSAS. SOMEBODY ONCE SAW HIM BUYING A PASTRAMI SANDWICH IN GERMANY. WHEN JERRY GLANVILLE COACHED THE ATLANTA FALCONS FOOTBALL TEAM, HE'D ALWAYS LEAVE A TICKET FOR ELVIS AT THE STADIUM. IN OTTAWA, ONTARIO, THERE'S EVEN AN OFFICIAL ELVIS SIGHTING SOCIETY. SADLY, ELVIS IS GONE. THE WAY HE REMAINS ALIVE IS IN HIS SONGS.

# TIMELINE OF ELVIS'S LIFE

1935 — Elvis is born in Tupelo, Mississippi

1946 — Gladys buys her son, Elvis, his first guitar

1948 — The Presleys move to Memphis

1953 — With $3.98 to pay for the session, Elvis records his first song, "My Happiness" at Sun Studios

1955 — RCA Records buys Elvis's contract from Sam Phillips for a then-record forty thousand dollars, plus a five-thousand-dollar bonus; Elvis soon records "Heartbreak Hotel"

1956 — *Love Me Tender*, Elvis's first movie, is released

1957 — Elvis buys Graceland, a mansion, for his family; Elvis is drafted into the U.S. Army

1958 — Gladys Presley dies

1960 — Elvis makes a comeback on a television special hosted by Frank Sinatra

1967 — Elvis and Priscilla get married

1968 — Lisa Marie Presley is born; Elvis stars in the television special that marks another comeback

1969 — Elvis returns to the concert stage in Las Vegas

1970 — President Richard Nixon meets Elvis at the White House

1973 — Elvis and Priscilla are divorced

1977 — On June 16, Elvis plays what will be his last concert; Elvis dies on August 16

# TIMELINE OF THE WORLD

Franklin D. Roosevelt wins the presidential election for the second time — 1936

Adolf Hitler of Germany invades Poland; World War II begins — 1939

The U.S. joins the Allied Forces in World War II in December — 1941

The U.S. drops an atomic bomb on the Japanese cities of Hiroshima and Nagasaki; World War II ends — 1945

The Supreme Court puts an end to separate schools for white children and black children — 1954

Black college students in North Carolina begin sit-ins at lunch counters that won't serve them — 1960

President John F. Kennedy is shot and killed in November — 1963

Color TV becomes popular in U.S. homes; the Beatles become a hit in the United States, starting the "British Invasion" of rock music — 1964

In October there is a huge protest against the Vietnam War in Washington, D.C. — 1967

Dr. Martin Luther King, Jr., is shot and killed in April; Senator Robert F. Kennedy is shot and killed in June — 1968

U.S. astronauts land on the moon in July; the Woodstock music festival takes place in August in upstate New York — 1969

President Richard M. Nixon resigns in August — 1974

## BIBLIOGRAPHY

Bret, David. **Elvis: The Hollywood Years**. Robson Books, London, 2001.

Esposito, Tony, and Elena Oumano. **Good Rockin' Tonight: Twenty Years on the Road and on Tour with Elvis**. Simon & Schuster, New York, 1994.

Guralnick, Peter. **Careless Love: The Unmaking of Elvis Presley**. Little, Brown and Company, Boston, 1999.

Guralnick, Peter. **Last Train to Memphis: The Rise of Elvis Presley**. Little, Brown and Company, Boston, 1994.

Hammontree, Patsy Guy. **Elvis Presley, A Bio-Bibliography**. Greenwood Press, Westport, CT, 1985.

Krogh, Egil "Bud." **The Day Elvis Met Nixon**. Pejama Press, Bellevue, WA, 1994.

Juanico, June. **Elvis: In the Twilight of Memory**. Arcade Publishing, New York, 1997.

Mason, Bobbie Ann. **Elvis Presley**. Lipper/Viking, New York, 2003.

O'Neal, Sean. **Elvis Inc.: The Fall and Rise of the Presley Empire**. Prima Publishing, Rocklin, CA, 1996.

Osborne, Jerry. **Elvis—Word for Word**. Harmony Books, New York, 1999.

Ritz, David. **Elvis by the Presleys**. Crown Publishers, New York, 2005.

Schroer, Andreas. **Private Presley: The Missing Years—Elvis in Germany**. William Morrow, New York, 1993.